Break

Tran

Your 7-Day Guide to Releasing God's Power!

Mike Van Buskirk

This resource is a personalized compilation of the following versions of the Bible:
American Standard Version
Copyright © 1901 by Public Domain,
GOD'S WORD Translation (GW)
Copyright © 1995 by God's Word to the Nations.
New King James Version
Copyright © 1982 by Thomas Nelson, Inc.
King James Version (KJV)
by Public Domain,
Young's Literal Translation (YLT)
by Public Domain,
New International Version, NIV®
Copyright © 1973, 1978, 1984, 2011 by Biblica, Inc.®,
Amplified Bible (AMP)
Copyright © 1954, 1958, 1962, 1964, 1965, 1987
by The Lockman Foundation

Each verse has been tailored specifically for the purpose of personal confession, and recorded, for the most part, in the first person.

Visit our website:

http://www.soul-purpose.org

Contact Info:

In the US write:

Soul Purpose Ministries
PO Box 51283
Eugene OR 97405 USA

In India:

Soul Purpose Ministries
PO Box 63
Gangtok Sikkim
India 737101

SOUL PURPOSE MINISTRIES
office@soul-purpose.org

Dedication

Breakfast With Jesus
was humbly assembled to the
glory of the Word, Who became
flesh and dwelt among us—
Our Mighty Lord and Savior,
Jesus Christ!

Endorsements

"I would highly recommend this book to anyone wanting to accelerate their growth in the Lord in a very deliberate way. This book is a great tool for both new and mature Christians who want to know, in a very practical way, how to take the power of God's Word and infuse it into their daily lives."

Daryl Boucher
www.wflministries.com
Eugene, Oregon USA

"Mike Van Buskirk has done us all a great service by giving us such an easy way to do such a powerful thing: speaking the Word of God over our lives! The regular confession of God's Word has produced more lasting change in my life than anything else. I gladly recommend this book to you. Not only read it, but use it consistently until speaking God's Word becomes automatic and your life is enriched by it's fruit."

Hayne Schurz
Missions Pastor
http://www.woctulsa.org
Tulsa, Oklahoma USA

"Nutritionists stress the importance of starting every day with a balanced Breakfast. Giving your body all it needs to start the day strong and alert. If that is true for our bodies, how much more our spirits. *Breakfast With Jesus* is one of those day starters that deposit all you need to start your day spiritually strong and alert. Pastor Mike Van Buskirk, by the Holy Spirit, has served up, not only Spiritual nutrition out of the Word of God, but has done it in such a way that each morning you can have *Breakfast With Jesus.*

Thanks Mike for putting together such a great way to start our day. Reader, enjoy every morning with Him."

Brian Cuff
Lead Pastor
www.harvesteugene.org
Eugene Oregon USA

Forward XI

Introduction XV

Instructions XVII

Day One

   THE WORD *19*

Day Two

   THE SPIRIT *23*

Day Three

   MY WALK *27*

Day Four

   MY MINISTRY *31*

Day Five

   HEALING *35*

Day Six

   PROSPERITY *39*

Day Seven

   THE HARVEST *43*

EPILOGUE & Free offer 47

About Soul Purpose 49

Forward

This is an amazing little booklet. I hate to even call it a booklet, meaning small book. This small book is so full of life that it deserves a much grander title . . . *Le Grande Book Extraordinaire,* perhaps. I think if we could see it in the spirit, we would see that it is glowing with the life of God.

Jesus Christ said, *"All things are possible to him who believes."* He wasn't having a Hallmark moment when He said this. He was speaking absolute, power-filled truth, which anyone can participate with and enjoy a life of supernatural provision.

But why do we need to "believe?"

Because, generally speaking, we cannot see the realm of the spirit. We cannot see our own spirits, or the Spirit of Christ that dwells within us. Though the Kingdom of God is the greater realm, and has the ability to override the natural realm, we cannot see it with our natural eyes. We must access that realm and it's resources by faith.

So how do we get faith?

Well, Hebrews 11:1 says, *"Faith comes by hearing and hearing by the Word of God."* Pretty simple concept . . . as spirits created in His image, when we hear the Word of God, our hearts resonate with His absolute truth and faith arises in us. Pretty exciting, but there is more.

Proverbs 18:21says, *Death and life are in the power of the tongue, and those who love it will eat its fruit.* What that means is that we can activate life with our words, and enjoy that life. We can, in faith, speak the Word of God, and it will release the supernatural realm to change the natural realm. As one preacher said, *Heaven is voice activated.*

So where do we begin? What do we say?

We say the Word of God! When we speak the Word of God, God acts. In Isaiah 55:11 He says, *"So shall My word be that goes forth from My mouth; It shall not return to Me void, But it shall accomplish what I please, And it shall prosper in the thing for which I sent it."* You might think, yah, but that is God, He can speak and have it come to pass because He is the Creator, but I'm just a beat-up, broken down person. Well, no my friend, your lack does not let you off the hook. In fact, it is your incentive to be Christ-like and speak words of life over your life.

Jesus taught us this in Mark 11:23-24, *"For assuredly, I say to You, whoever says to this mountain, 'Be removed and be cast into the sea,' and does not doubt in his heart, but believes that those things he says will be done, he will have whatever he says. Therefore I say to you, whatever things you ask when you pray, believe that you receive them, and you will have them.*" Just like God speaks and His words come to pass and do not return to Him void, *we* are supposed to speak words that come to pass and do not return to *us* void, or powerless, or without accomplishing the things they were sent out to do.

Notice in the above verses that the "asking" to which Jesus is referring is actually *declaring* or *commanding*. In essence, Jesus said, *whoever commands a mountain to be removed, will receive a mountain removed.* He didn't say whoever gets on their knees and humbly cries out to the Lord for help, to move the mountain, will get a yes answer. No! We are to boldly declare and command the mountains of our lives to move. There are times and places to supplicate, to ask God for wisdom and direction, but there are also times to declare boldly.

We have the great privilege of declaring life over our lives, and we do so by declaring the Word of God. His Word is life. It contains everything we could ever need, and when we declare His Word in faith, His Grace is activated and His power is released to fulfill His Word, and conform our lives to the Word, which we spoke. If there is no need, there is no need to speak. It is because you have need that you must speak! This is not a game for the elite. The more broken you are, the more you must speak.

And this brings us to *Breakfast With Jesus*. With the idea of declaring the Word of God on specific subjects, Mike Van Buskirk has compiled seven collections of power filled Scripture for us to declare. These declarations are filled with the life of God, and I am in love with this book. It is so precious to me. When I look at it, here beside me, it is like looking at a jewelry box full of sparkling jewels of life that release miracles.

Mike has done a stellar job of collecting Scripture related to specific areas of provision for our lives. When you begin to read them, you will immediately begin to feel the life they contain. When you declare them, you will feel that life being released. You will know in your heart that something supernatural is happening and that your life will never be the same.

If you need a miracle, or miracles, in your life—if you need your life to look completely different than it currently looks, then you will take this book and you will run, not walk, to the nearest quiet place and immediately begin to implement the declarations contained within its pages. I encourage you to do so with the heart of a warrior.

Have you seen the movie Brave Heart? Imagine your face painted blue, and you are on a horse, and you have the sword of the Lord in Your hand, and you are charging into battle with the Word of God as Your weapon! Declare these words with a brave heart! Declare them with courage and dignity. Declare them with authority!

When you do so, God, Who honors His Word and keeps His promises, will cause these Words to become living fruit in your life and you *will* eat that fruit. You, and Your life, *will* be transformed. This is not a "Well, maybe . . ." situation. No! This is as true as truth ever gets. You have life in the power of your tongue. Wield that weapon! Release miracles into your life with faith filled words from the Word of God. Begin with the powerful declarations Mike has collected and let this become a lifestyle for you, one of speaking life and receiving life. You will never be the same.

Donna Crow
Fountain of Life Healing School
http://www.DonnaCrow.com

Introduction

I figure the chances are fairly good that you've picked up this resource and opened its pages during some morning, perhaps before or after breakfast? And you've made a good decision, one that I pray will last you a lifetime. Over the years, I've seen the amazing difference the Word of God can make in a persons life; I am one of those lives, and I've seen countless individuals touched and changed—literally transformed by the power of God's Word.

Sadly, I've also seen countless individuals remain the same, seemingly unchanged while being exposed to the same powerful truths. The difference lies in the response. Two people can hear the same message, but the only one who will be impacted is the one who takes that message personally.

The Word of God will make as much of a difference in our lives as we allow it to. The extent to which we give it our earnest attention and cooperate with it, will determine the heights and depths of our life. How high do you want to go? How deep?

There is no end to the revelation of wisdom and knowledge that flow forth from the pages of the most powerful document known to man, the Bible. God's Holy Word is without a doubt the single most life-transforming document in existence. It is important that we don't take it lightly, and don't make any excuse for why it won't work in our life.

God's Word knows no socioeconomic boundaries; it works regardless of geography. Any people, of any land, can experience the power of God's Word in their lives, and that includes you. God is no respecter of persons; He doesn't choose to bless some, and leave others out. No, He has made the means of receiving an inheritance available to all. The problem comes when individuals are ignorant of their inheritance, n o t k n o w i n g what belongs to them. The words of God recorded in Hosea 4:6 become true, *"My people are destroyed for lack of knowledge."*

It's up to us to know all we can about the wonderful treasures God has made available to us. The Word of God is the storehouse of His treasure, and we can only receive from Him what we know has been made available by Him.

As you continue to partake of God's divine nature, by and

through the precious promises that He has made available to you, and as you continue to increase in the knowledge of God, you will become a mighty force for God in the earth. Great and mighty things will be accomplished through your life, for God's glory!

It is my prayer that the following pages will help you to draw closer to God through His Word. I encourage you to use the following daily declarations to keep the Word of God in your mouth and in your heart, and ask the Lord to give you wisdom to act on His Word. May your life never be the same as you take time to have *Breakfast with Jesus*. Or, if you choose, make it brunch, lunch or dinner.

Time well spent is never lost, but rather invested, and what better investment could you make than time with the Lord? Enjoy.

Mike Van Buskirk

Instructions

Though these declarations are formatted for use one day at a time, feel free to be creative.

You may find that you want to do several days of declarations on the same day. Or, you might want to pick particular declarations out that seem most alive to you in the moment.

Keep in mind that these are not Christian incantations. No! This is the living Word of God, brought to a focused point for the purpose of declaring life in a focused way. This bears fruit when it is done in faith, with confidence in the God of Creation who keeps His promises. Vain repetition of the Word of God from your flesh will not bear fruit.

Meditate on these scriptures. Let them come alive in your heart, and then boldly declare them in faith and expect the Word of God to bear fruit in your life.

Though these declarations are based on Scripture, you will find your faith increases even more when you look up the verses listed in the References. To enjoy them in various translations, in parallel, you can visit http://www.bible.cc. There, you can type in any Bible verse reference, such as John 3:16, and their online program will open that verse in more than 20 different translations of the Bible. This is a free service and we think you will enjoy it.

Numbers 14:28 says, "Say to them, 'As I live,' says the LORD, 'just as you have spoken in My hearing, so I will surely do to you . . .'"

The time to speak life is now!

Day One

THE WORD

The Gospel of John, chapter one and verse one, begins with these words, *"...in the beginning was the Word..."* and it is this place of beginning that I want to note first. God describes His beginning with His Word, and we can also allow God's Word to become the description of our beginning by giving it first place each day. God's mighty Word is the best beginning to any day, and if you will take the time to give it first place in your life, you will reap the bountiful benefits of it working in your life.

For the next seven days, I want to encourage you to use the following seven confession of God's mighty Word to start your day. As you allow the Word of God to work in your life by confessing it, you will see the difference it makes. Truly the Word of God is living and powerful, and when its power is activated in your life, things change. Make active the power of God's Word today by opening your mouth and speaking it boldly over you life. Ready, get set, Go!

---

[1]*God's Word* is sure; therefore I do well to take heed, as unto a lamp shining in a dark place, until the day dawns, and the day-star rises in my heart: Knowing this first, that no *prophecy of scripture* is of any private interpretation. For no prophecy ever came by the will of man: but men spoke from God, being moved by the Holy Spirit. [2]How can I keep my life pure? I can do it by holding on to *the Word*. [3]I have treasured *Your promise* in my heart so that I may not sin against You. [4]I will meditate on *Your Word*, and fix my eyes on *Your ways*. [5]Open my eyes, that I may behold wondrous things out of *Your Word*. [6] I will not live by bread alone, but by every *Word* that proceeds out of the mouth of God. [7]The bread of God is He Who comes down from Heaven and gives life to the world. [8]If I abide in You and *Your Words* abide in me, I can ask

for anything I want, and it will be mine.

⁹*The Word* is near me, in my mouth and in my heart (that is, *the Word of faith* which I proclaim).

¹⁰Faith comes by hearing, and hearing by the *Word of God*.

¹¹I am sanctified and cleansed with the washing of water by *the Word*.

¹²Through faith I understand that the worlds were framed by *the Word of God*, so that things, which are seen, were not made of things which do appear.

¹³For the *Word of God* is living and full of power and is sharper than any two-edged sword, cutting through and making a division even of the soul and the spirit, the bones and the muscles, and is quick to see the thoughts and purposes of the heart.

¹⁴By the *word of the Lord* were the heavens made; and all the host of them by the breath of His mouth.

¹⁵Forever, O LORD, *Your Word* is firmly fixed in the heavens.

¹⁶Heaven and earth shall pass away: but *Your Words* shall not pass away.

¹⁷*Your Word* burns in my heart and bones, and I cannot keep silent.

¹⁸*Your Word* is like fire, and like a hammer, smashing the rock to bits?

¹⁹I will worship toward Your holy temple, and give thanks unto Your name for Your loving kindness and for *Your truth*: For You have magnified *Your Word* above Your entire name.

²⁰*Your Word* is a lamp for my feet and a light for my path.

²¹In the beginning was *the Word*, and *the Word* was with God, and *the Word* was God.

²²I praise *the Word* of God. I trust God. I am not afraid. What can mere flesh and blood do to me?

²³Every *Word of God* has proven to be true. He is a shield to those who come to Him for protection.

²⁴The grass withers, the flower fades; but the *Word of our God* shall stand forever.

²⁵I take up the helmet of salvation, and the sword of the Spirit, which is *God's Word*; praying at all seasons, with all prayer and supplication in the Spirit, and watching unto this very thing with all perseverance and supplication for all the saints; praying at the same time also, that God may open to me a door for *the Word*, to speak the secret of the Christ.

²⁶The *Word of the LORD* is perfect, reviving my soul;

the *Word of the LORD* is sure, making me wise; the *Word's of the LORD* are right, rejoicing my heart; the *Word of the LORD* is pure, enlightening my eyes; the fear of the LORD is clean, enduring forever; the *Word's of the LORD* are true, and righteous altogether. They are more desirable than gold, even the finest gold. They are sweeter than honey, even the drippings from a honeycomb.

27*God's Word*, which goes out of His mouth; it shall not return to Him void, but it shall accomplish that which He pleases, and it shall prosper in what He sent it to do!

28The disciples spread the Good News everywhere, and the Lord worked with them. He confirmed *His Word* with miraculous signs. 29 Then the LORD has said, "I am watching over *my Word* to perform it."

30Bless the LORD, O You His angels, you mighty ones who do *His Word*, hearkening to the voice of *His Word*! I give voice to *God's Word*. *God's Word* is working in my life, *His Word* is coming to pass; it is bearing fruit, 31 100 fold in my life.

32*God's Word* is renewing me, transforming me, and making me like Jesus. My life is being changed.

33 I'm going from glory to glory, 34and from faith to faith. 35I'm rooted, and grounded. 36I'm built on the rock; 37 I will not be shaken! In the name of Jesus, Amen!

_____

References:
_____

1 2 Peter 1:19-21
2 Psalm 119:9
3 Psalm 119:11
4 Psalm 119:15
5 Psalm 119:18
6 Matthew 4:4
7 John 6:33
8 John 15:7
9 Romans 10:8
10 Romans 10:17
11 Ephesians 5:26
12 Hebrews 11:3
13 Hebrews 4:12
14 Psalm 33:6
15 Psalm 119:89
16 Matthew 24:35
17 Jeremiah 20:9
18 Jeremiah 23:29
19 Psalm 138:2
20 Psalm 119:105
21 John 1:1
22 Psalm 56:4
23 Proverbs 30:5
24 Isaiah 40:8
25 Ephesians 6:17-19
26 Psalm 19:7-10
27 Isaiah 55:11
28 Mark 16:20
29 Jeremiah 1:12
30 Psalm 103:20
31 Matthew 13:23

32 Romans 12:2   35 Ephesians 3:17
33 2 Corinthians 3:18   36 Matthew 7:24
34 Romans 1:15-17   37 2 Thessalonians 2:2

NOTES:_____

_____
_____
_____
_____
_____
_____
_____
_____
_____
_____
_____
_____
_____
_____
_____
_____
_____
_____
_____
_____
_____
_____
_____

Day Two

THE SPIRIT

A good rule to live by is to put the Word first, and to put the Spirit second. The Spirit of God is like a river, and every river requires a riverbed to flow within. Once the riverbed of God's Word is established in our lives, the Spirit of God can flow freely within its borders.

---

[1]My heart stirs me this day; The *Holy Spirit* makes me willing.

[2]The Lord will never leave me nor forsake me;

[3]He will never take *His Spirit* from me.

[4]The Lord is with those of a contrite and humble spirit, to revive the spirit of the humble, and to revive the heart of the contrite ones. I am revived, and I live in revival.

[5]I will not vex, [6]grieve, [7]or quench the *Holy Spirit*.

[8]I have asked my Father to give me *His Spirit,* and He has.

[9]I've been baptized with the *Holy Spirit* and with fire.

[10]I've been filled with the *Holy Spirit,* and I speak in other tongues.

[11]I believe, and I have been sealed with the *Holy Spirit* of promise.

[12]The Lord is bringing revelation to me by *His Spirit.*

[13]The Lord speaks through me by *His Spirit.*

[14]The *Holy Ghost* is my:
Comforter,
Counselor,
Helper,
Intercessor,
Advocate,
Strengthener, and
Standby.

He teaches me all things, and He brings all things to my remembrance.

[15]The *Spirit of truth*; dwells with me, and lives on the inside of me. [16]He abides with me forever.

[17]I received power to be a witness when the *Holy Spirit* came and filled me.

[18]I walk in the comfort of the *Holy Spirit.* [19]God has anointed me with *His Spirit* and with power: that I may do good, and bring healing to all who are oppressed of the devil.

[20] The *Holy Spirit* speaks

to me.

²¹The *Holy Spirit* sends me forth.

²²I am filled with joy, and the *Holy Ghost*.

²³The *Holy Ghost* has shed the love of God abroad in my heart.

²⁴My conscious also bears me witness in the *Holy Ghost*.

²⁵ For the kingdom of God is not meat and drink; but righteousness, and peace, and joy in the *Holy Ghost*.

²⁶The God of hope has filled me with all joy and peace in believing, that I may abound in hope, through the power of the *Holy Ghost*.

²⁷The *Holy Sprit* is teaching me.

²⁸ My body is the temple of the *Holy Spirit*, I am not my own. I've been bought with a price; the precious blood of Jesus: therefore I glorify God in my body, and in my spirit, which are God's.

²⁹The grace of the Lord Jesus, and the love of God, and the communion and sharing together, and participation of the *Holy Spirit* is with me.

³⁰I keep the good things, which have been committed to me by the *Holy Ghost* Who dwells in me.

³¹The *Holy Spirit* is renewing me.

³² I hear *His* voice today.

³³ I build myself up on my most holy faith, praying in the *Holy Ghost*.

³⁴I worship in spirit and I worship in truth.

³⁵The comforter has come, even the *Spirit of Truth*, He is guiding me into all truth:

³⁶ He is not speaking on His own, but whatever He hears, that He will speak: and He is showing, announcing, and disclosing unto me the things that are to come, that will happen in the future.

³⁷My soul has been purified, through the *Spirit*, in obeying the truth.

³⁸ When the enemy comes in like a flood, the *Spirit of the Lord* shall lift up a standard against him.

³⁹With an open face I behold as in a glass the glory of the Lord, I am being changed into the same image from glory to glory, even as by the *Spirit of the Lord*.

⁴⁰I have the spirit of wisdom and revelation in the knowledge of God. The eyes of my understanding have been enlightened; that I may know what is the hope of His calling, and what are the riches of His inheritance in the saints, and what is the exceeding greatness of His power toward me as a believer, according to the working of His might power,

which He wrought in Christ, when He raised Him from the dead, and set Him at His own right hand in the heavenly places.

⁴¹Grant me, according to the riches of Your glory, to be strengthened with might by *Your Spirit* in my inner man, that Christ may dwell in my heart by faith; that I, being rooted and grounded in love, may be able to comprehend with all the saints what is the breadth, and length, and depth, and height, that I may know the love of Christ, which passes knowledge, that I may be filled with all the fullness of God. He is able to do exceedingly abundantly above all that I ask or think, according to the power that is at work in me.

⁴²The *Spirit of Glory* and of God rests upon me. ⁴³ The fruit of *God's Spirit* inside my spirit is love,

> joy,
> peace,
> patience,
> gentleness,
> goodness,
> faith,
> meekness,
> and temperance,

against such there in no law. ⁴⁴The fruit of the *Spirit* is in all goodness and righteousness and truth.

⁴⁵I am Christ's and I have crucified the flesh with its affections and lusts. I live in the *Spirit*, and I walk in the *Spirit*.

⁴⁶I pray with the *Spirit*, and I sing with the *Spirit*.

⁴⁷I'm not drunk with wine, but I'm filled with the *Spirit*: I speak with psalms and hymns and spiritual songs, I sing and make melody in my heart to the Lord. I give thanks always and for all things unto God and my Father in the name of my Lord Jesus Christ.

⁴⁸The law of the *Spirit of life* in Christ Jesus has made me free from the law of sin and death.

⁴⁹The righteousness of the law has been fulfilled in me, for I do not walk after the flesh, but after the *Spirit*. For they that are of the flesh do mind the things of the flesh; but I'm after the *Spirit*, and I mind the things of the *Spirit*. I am not carnally minded; but I'm spiritually minded leading to life and peace.

⁵⁰I am a child of God, and the *Spirit of God* leads me. I have not received the spirit of bondage to fear; but I have received the *Spirit of adoption*, whereby I cry, Abba, Father. The *Holy Spirit* bears witness with my spirit, that I am a child of God.

⁵¹The *Holy Spirit* helps me in my weakness: for even

if I do not know what I should pray, or how I should pray: the *Spirit Himself* makes intercession for me as I pray in the *Spirit*. [52]I do not have a spirit of fear; but of power and love, and a sound mind.

In the name of Jesus, Amen!

References:

1 Exodus 35:21
2 Hebrews 13:5
3 Psalm 51:11
4 Isaiah 57:15
5 Isaiah 63:10
6 Ephesians 4:30
7 1 Thessalonians 5:19
8 Luke 11:13
9 Matthew 3:11
10 Acts 2:4
11 Ephesians 1:13
12 Ephesians 4:30
13 Mark 13:11
14 John 14:26
15 John 17:17
16 John 14:16
17 Acts 1:8
18 Acts 9:31
19 Acts 10:38
20 Acts 13:2
21 Acts 13:4
22 Acts 13:52
23 Romans 5:5
24 Romans 9:1
25 Rom. 14:17
26 Romans 15:13
27 1 Cor. 2:13
28 1 Cor. 6:19-20
29 2 Cor. 13:14
30 2 Tim. 1:14
31 Titus 3:5
32 Hebrews 3:7
33 Jude 1:20
34 John 4:23
35 John 15:26
36 John 16:13
37 1 Peter 1:22
38 Isaiah 59:19
39 2 Cor. 3:18
40 Eph. 1:17-20
41 Eph. 3:16-21
42 1 Peter 4:14
43 Gal. 5:22-25
44 Eph. 5:9
45 Gal. 5:24
46 1 Cor. 14:15
47 Eph. 5:18-20
48 Romans 8:2
49 Rom. 8:4-6
60 Rom 8:14-16
51 Romans 8:26
52 2 Tim. 1:7

NOTES:_____

_____
_____
_____
_____
_____

Day Three

MY WALK

With the Word of God and the Spirit of God, you are equipped and empowered to touch the world for God! The way you touch the world around you will be determined by your walk with God.

---

[1]In pastures of tender grass You cause me to lie down, by quiet waters You lead me. You refresh my soul; You lead me in paths of righteousness for Your names sake. Even though *I walk through* the dark valley of death, because You are with me, I fear no harm. Your rod and Your staff give me comfort and courage. You arrange a table before me, over-against my adversaries, You have anointed my head with oil, my cup runs over! Only goodness and kindness pursue me, all the days of my life, and my dwelling is in the house of Jehovah, for a length of days!

[2]Examine me, O Lord, and test me. Look closely into my heart and mind. I see Your mercy and lovingkindness in front of me. *I walk* in the light of Your truth. I do not sit with liars, and I will not be found among hypocrites.

[3]But *I walk* with integrity. My feet stand on level ground.

[4]With You *I can walk* over my enemies. With Your Name I can trample those who attack me.

[5]You have rescued me from death. You have kept my feet from stumbling so that I can *walk* in Your Presence, in the light of life.

[6]Righteousness and justice are the foundation of Your throne. Mercy and truth go before You.

[7]*I will walk* in Your Presence in this world of the living.

[8]*I will walk* around freely because I seek out Your guiding principles.

[9]Even though I may be in the middle of trouble, You will revive me and keep me alive. You guard my life against the anger of my enemies. You stretch out Your hand, and Your right hand saves me.

¹⁰You have reserved priceless wisdom for me. You are a shield for me because I *walk in integrity.* You guard those on paths of justice and watch over the way of Your godly ones.

¹¹*When I walk,* my stride will not be hampered. Even if I run, I will not stumble.

¹²I will not stray onto the path of wickedness. *I will not walk* in the way of evil. I avoid it, and I do not *walk* near it.

¹³ I carefully *walk a straight path,* and all my ways are secure. I'll not lean to the right or to the left. I *walk away* from evil.

¹⁴I obey the commands of my Father; I do not forsake the teaching of my mother; I fasten them on my heart forever. I hang them around my neck. When *I walk* around, they will lead me. When I lie down, they will watch over me. When I wake up, they will talk to me because the command is a lamp, the teachings are light, and the warnings from discipline are the path of life.

¹⁵ My strength is renewed for I wait in hope for the Lord. I will soar with wings like eagles. I will run and won't become weary. I will *walk* and won't grow tired.

¹⁶The Spirit of the one Who brought Jesus back to life lives in me! That same Spirit gives supernatural life to my body now.

¹⁷Since I have these promises of God, I cleanse my self from everything that contaminates body and spirit and I live a holy life in the fear of my God.

¹⁸My Father knew me long ago and chose me to live a holy life, with the Spirit's help, so that I am obedient to Jesus and am sprinkled with His blood. Grace and Peace are mine in fullest measure.

¹⁹I choose to obey Christ's commands and I live in God, and God lives in me. I know that He lives in me because He has given me His Sprit.

²⁰*I walk in the Spirit,* and I will not fulfill the lust of the flesh.

²¹I have the mind of Christ,

²²and my body is a living sacrifice, acceptable to God.

²³I have been crucified with Christ, it's no longer I, who live, but Christ Who lives in me; and this life that I live in the flesh, I live by faith in the Son of God Who loved me and gave Himself for me.

²⁴I *walk by faith,* not by sight.

²⁵And, I *walk in love,* as Christ also has loved me, and

has given Himself for me as an offering and a sacrifice to God. [26]And this is love that I *walk* after His commandments. This is the commandment, that, as I have heard from the beginning, and I *walk* in it. [27] I am patient. I am kind. I am not jealous. I don't sing my own praises. I am not arrogant. I am not rude. I don't seek my own. I'm not irritable or provoked. I don't keep track of wrongs that others do. I'm never glad with sin, but always glad to side with the truth. I never stop being patient, never stop believing, never stop hoping, and I never give up! God's love in me will never fail, and never come to an end. [28] I eagerly pursue this love; I make it my quest in life to lay hold of it. It is my aim, and it is my guide. [29]My steps are ordered of the Lord; He delights in my way [30]and favor surrounds me like a shield. [31]I do nothing out of selfish ambition or vain conceit, but in humility of heart I count others as more excellent than myself. [32]I *walk in the light*, as He is in the light, I have fellowship with others, and the blood of Jesus Christ cleanses me of all sin.

In the name of Jesus, Amen!

References:

---

1 Psalm 23:2-6
2 Psalm 26:2-4
3 Psalm 26:11-12
4 Psalm 44:5
5 Psalm 56:13
6 Psalm 89:14
7 Psalm 116:9
8 Psalm 119:45
9 Psalm 138:7
10 Proverbs 2:7-8
11 Proverbs 4:12
12 Prov. 4:14-15
13 Prov. 4:26-27
14 Prov. 6:20-23
15 Isaiah 40:31
16 Romans 8:11
17 2 Corinthians 7:1
18 1 Peter 1:2
19 1 John 3:24
20 Galatians 5:16
21 1 Corinthians 2:16
22 Romans 12:1
23 Galatians 2:20
24 2 Corinthians 5:7
25 Ephesians 5:2
26 2 John 1:6
27 1 Corinthians 13:4-8
28 1 Corinthians 14:1
29 Psalm 37:23
30 Psalm 5:12
31 Philippians 2:3
32 1 John 1:7

NOTES:_____

_____

_____

_____

_____

_____

_____

_____

_____

_____

_____

_____

_____

_____

_____

_____

_____

_____

_____

_____

_____

_____

_____

_____

_____

_____

_____

_____

_____

_____

_____

Day Four

MY MINISTRY

We've focused on the Word of God, the Spirit of God, our Walk with God, and now our Ministry.

Do you know that God has a ministry for you to fulfill? God has called you to do great things for Him; He is faithful to equip you with everything you need to accomplish His plan.

The wonderful equipment that God has supplied us with is laid up in His Word, just waiting for us to discover it. As you continue to meditate on the mighty Word of God, and confess His promises over your life, His equipping becomes yours!

---

¹I am a *minister* of the New Covenant ²a *minister* of the Spirit;

³I have this treasure in an earthen vessel and the excellency of the power is of God not me.

⁴He has *called* me with a holy calling, not according to my works, but according to His own purpose and grace.

⁵I shine as a light in the world, and I am salt in the earth.

⁶His purpose will be fulfilled in me.

⁷I will run *my race* with endurance, ⁸and I will finish *my course;* ⁹looking unto Jesus, the author and the finisher of my faith. ¹⁰He has begun a good work in me, and it will come to full completion.

¹¹No weapon formed against me will prosper, ¹²for I am more than a conqueror through Him Who strengthens me.

¹³All things are possible for me, because I believe.

¹⁴I believe, and it shall be even as it's been told me.

¹⁵I'm a *soul winner,* ¹⁶and a *miracle worker.*

¹⁷I do the work of an *evangelist.*

¹⁸I do the works of Jesus, and even greater works because the Holy Ghost lives in me.

¹⁹I lay hands on the sick

and they recover - I cast out devils in the name of Jesus - and nothing shall by any means hurt me.

²⁰I trample on snakes and scorpions, and over all the power of the enemy.

²¹Favor surrounds me like a shield.

²²I have favor with God, and I have favor with men.

²³My *gift* makes room for me, and brings me before great men.

²⁴I will do *great exploits* for God.

²⁵I ask for the nations.

²⁶I am an *ambassador for Christ* - God is pleading through me for the world to be reconciled. ²⁷I will proclaim boldly the truth of the gospel.

²⁸I am not ashamed of the gospel. It is the power of God unto salvation. *Power is released when I preach the good news of Jesus.*

²⁹I have power to be a *witness*; ³⁰and woe is me if I don't preach the gospel.

³¹I will become all things to all men that I may by all means *save some.*

³²I will gladly spend and be spent for *souls.*

³³I will go into all the world and preach the gospel, ³⁴and I will *make disciples* in all nations. *I'm on a mission from God.*

³⁵I don't entangle myself with the affairs of this life;

³⁶I keep myself pure and free that I may set others free.

³⁷Since I have, in obedience to the truth, purified my soul, I can fervently love others from my heart.

³⁸I keep that which has been committed to me,

³⁹and I guard my heart above all things. I put away false and dishonest speech; I put willful and contrary talk far from me. My eyes look directly ahead, and my gaze is straight before me. I consider well the path of my feet, and all my ways are established and ordered aright. I turn not aside to the right hand or to the left; I remove my foot from evil.

⁴⁰Out of my inner most being flows rivers of living water.

⁴¹There is a well of salvation on the inside of me, and I draw water from it joyfully.

⁴²Thank You Father for sending me, ⁴³and choosing me to bear fruit for eternity.

⁴⁴I am a vessel of honor, sanctified and useful for You; prepared for every good work.

⁴⁵I am a *workman* that doesn't need to be ashamed, ⁴⁶making full proof of my *ministry.* I will do all that I've been called to do!

[47]Lacking no good things, [48]and possessing an abundance for every good work.

[49]And I thank Christ Jesus our Lord, Who strengthens me, because He counted me faithful, putting me into the *ministry*.

In the name of Jesus, Amen!

References:

---

1 2 Corinthians 3:6
2 2 Corinthians 3:8
3 2 Corinthians 4:7
4 2 Timothy 1:9
5 Matthew 5:13,14
6 Psalm 138:8
7 Hebrews 12:1
8 2 Timothy 4:7
9 Hebrews 12:2
10 Philippians 1:6
11 Isaiah 54:17
12 Romans 8:37
13 Mark 9:23
14 Acts 27:25
15 Proverbs 11:30
16 Romans 15:18,19
   2 Corinthians 12:12
17 2 Timothy 4:5
18 John 14:12-17
19 Mark 16:17,18
20 Luke 10:19
21 Psalm 5:12
22 Proverbs 3:4
   Luke 2:52
23 Proverbs 18:16
24 Daniel 11:32
25 Psalm 2:8
26 2 Corinthians 5:20
27 Ephesians 6:19
28 Romans 1:16
29 Acts 1:8
30 1 Corinthians 9:16
31 1 Corinthians 9:19-22
32 2 Corinthians 12:15
33 Mark 16:15
34 Matthew 28:19
35 2 Timothy 2:4
36 1 John 3:3
37 1 Peter 1:22
38 1 Timothy 6:20
   2 Timothy 1:14
39 Proverbs 4:23-27
40 John 7:38
41 Isaiah 12:3
42 Isaiah 6:8
43 John 15:16
44 2 Timothy 2:21
45 2 Timothy 2:15
46 2 Timothy 4:5
47 Psalm 34:10
48 2 Corinthians 9:8
49 1 Timothy 1:12

NOTES:_____

_____

_____

_____

_____

NOTES:_____

_____
_____
_____
_____
_____
_____
_____
_____
_____
_____
_____
_____
_____
_____
_____
_____
_____
_____
_____
_____
_____
_____
_____
_____
_____
_____
_____
_____
_____
_____

Day Five

HEALING

Thank God for the Word of God! We have been thoroughly equipped to stand against the enemy and rise up victorious amidst any circumstance.

There are some specific areas that we need to make sure our faith is extra built up in, these are areas that the enemy continually attacks God's people in because he wants to hinder us from fulfilling the Great Commission. Our health is one of these areas, and Romans 10:17 says faith comes *by hearing the Word of God.* As we spend time feeding our faith regarding divine health, our faith shield will be reinforced and we will quench all the fiery darts of the devil. As we in faith declare the Word of God regarding our health, His grace is released to sustain us in complete physical wholeness.

---

¹I fear the name of the Lord, and the Sun of righteousness has risen with *healing* in His wings for me. I shall go forth, and grow up as a calf of the stall. I shall tread down the wicked; for they shall be ashes under the soles of my feet.

²Jesus went about all of Galilee, teaching in their synagogues, and preaching the gospel of the kingdom, and *healing* all manner of sickness and all manner of disease among the people.

³And the people followed Him: and He received them, and spoke unto them of the kingdom of God, and *healed* all who had need of *healing.*

⁴God anointed Jesus of Nazareth with the Holy Ghost and with power: Who went about doing good, and *healing* all that were oppressed of the devil; for God was with Him.

⁵Why are You cast down, oh my soul? And why are You disquieted within me? Hope in God: for I shall yet praise Him, Who is the *health* of my countenance,

⁶Be merciful unto me, and bless me; and cause Your face to shine upon me, that

Your way may be known upon the earth, Your *saving health* among all nations.

⁷My light breaks forth as the morning, and my *health springs forth* speedily: and my righteousness shall go before me; the glory of the Lord shall be my rearguard.

⁸The Lord has restored *health* unto me, He has *healed* all my wounds.

⁹The Lord brought me *health and cure,* He reveals His cure to me, and He continues to reveal unto me the abundance of peace and truth.

¹⁰I prosper in all things and I walk *in health,* even as my soul prospers.

¹¹I serve the Lord God, and He blesses my bread, and my water; and He *takes sickness away* from the midst of me.

¹²The Lord has taken away from me all sickness, and He puts no evil or disease upon me.

¹³The Lord *preserves* me, and keeps me alive; and I shall be blessed upon the earth; and I will not be delivered into the hands of my enemies.

¹⁴I lift my voice unto the Lord, and He *manifests healing* unto me.

¹⁵He sent His Word, and *healed* me, and delivered me from all destruction.

¹⁶He was wounded for my transgressions, He was bruised for my iniquities; the chastisement for my peace was upon Him; and with His stripes *I am healed.*

¹⁷You've *healed* me oh Lord, and I am *healed;* You've saved me, and I am saved; for You are my praise.

¹⁸It has come to pass, that every thing that lives, which moves, wherever the rivers shall come, shall live; and there is a very great multitude of fish, because these waters have come forth; for they shall be *healed*; and everything shall live wherever the river comes. The river has come to me, and I live in this river of life.

¹⁹The Lord Jesus' fame went throughout all the land; and they brought unto Him all sick people that were taken with different diseases and torments, and those who were possessed with devils, and those who were lunatic, and those that had the palsy; and He *healed* them all.

²⁰The Lord has but spoken the Word, and I've been *made whole.*

²¹As I believe, so is it done unto me.

²²All who come to Jesus for healing are made *whole.*

²³He *heals* the blind and the deaf.

²⁴He is moved with compassion and heals the sick.

²⁵He *heals* the lame, blind, mute, crippled, and all others who come to Him.

²⁶Whether it's an issue of blood, or any other plague, faith in Jesus makes us *whole.*

²⁷*Healing virtue* comes out of Jesus.

²⁸I give glory to God for my healing!

²⁹I'm not moved by what I see, but what I believe moves me.

³⁰I have faith for healing,

³¹and my faith has made me whole.

³²Healing belongs to me, it is the children's bread.

³³From the crown of my head, even to the soles of my feet

³⁴I am without disease and my *healing is complete,*

³⁵Romans 8 declares that God's Spirit in me gives life to my flesh and healing to my body. ³⁶So here I stand, completely *healthy and whole,* ³⁷here I stand without spot or wrinkle.

³⁸I am redeemed from the curse of sickness.

³⁹I resist the devil, the one who brings sickness, ⁴⁰and he must flee from me.

⁴¹I bless the Lord, and I remember His benefits; for it is He, Who forgives all my iniquities, and it is *He Who heals all my diseases.* He redeems my life from destruction and crowns me with loving kindness and tender mercies; He satisfies my mouth with good things, and my Youth is *renewed* like the eagles.

⁴²No plague shall come near my dwelling.

In the name of Jesus, Amen!

_____

References:

_____

1 Malachi 4:2

2 Matthew 4:23,
   Luke 9:6

3 Luke 9:11

4 Acts 10:38

5 Psalm 42:11

6 Psalm 67:1,2

7 Isaiah 58:8

8 Jeremiah 30:17

9 Jeremiah 33:6

10 3 John 1:2

11 Exodus 23:25

12 Deuteronomy 7:15

13 Psalm 41:2

14 Psalm 30:2

15 Psalm 107:20

16 Isaiah 53:5

17 Jeremiah 17:14

18 Ezekiel 47:9

19 Matthew 4:24

20 Matthew 8:8

21 Matt. 8:13, 8:16

22 Matthew 12:15

23 Matthew 12:22

24 Matthew 14:14
25 Matthew 15:30
26 Mark 5:29
27 Luke 6:19
28 Luke 17:15
29 2 Corinthians 5:7
30 Acts 14:9
31 Matthew 9:22,
   Mark 5:34,
   Luke 8:48
32 Matthew 15:26,
   Mark 7:27

33 2 Samuel 14:25
34 Psalm 103:3
35 Romans 8:11
36 Acts 4:10
37 Ephesians 5:27
38 Galatians 3:13
39 Acts 10:38
   John 10:10
40 James 4:7
41 Psalm 103:2-5
42 Psalm 91:10

NOTES:_____

_____

_____

_____

_____

_____

_____

_____

_____

_____

_____

_____

_____

_____

_____

_____

_____

_____

_____

_____

Day Six

PROSPERITY

Prosperity is another one of *those* areas, in which the enemy loves to attack the people of God. Satan knows if he can keep God's people in poverty and lack, or broke and in debt, that he can successfully hinder them from going into all the world with the gospel.

We cannot afford to live below the standards of God's blessing. His Word establishes that standard, and your words will cause you to rise to it. Get ready to be lifted higher, and higher, and higher!

---

¹Father, I thank You that You are with me, and that You make all that I do to *prosper* in my hand.

²I will keep Your Word, and Your Covenant, that I may continually *prosper* in all that I do.

³I *prosper* everywhere I go. I am strong, and I am courageous, and I will observe to do according to all that You have written.

⁴I *prosper* in all that I do, everywhere I go, and whichever way I turn, because I walk in Your ways, and keep Your word.

⁵Father, I thank You that as long as I seek You, You will make me to *prosper*.

⁶I am like a tree planted by the rivers of water. I bring forth my fruit in its season. My leaf does not wither, and whatever I do *prospers*.

⁷I pray for the peace of Jerusalem, I *prosper* because I love her.

⁸I *prosper* in all things, and I walk in health, even as my soul *prospers*.

⁹I will spend all my days in *prosperity*, and my years in pleasure because I love You, Lord.

¹⁰I shout for joy, and I am glad for I favor Your righteous cause. I say continually, be magnified, Oh Lord, You take pleasure in my *prosperity*.

¹¹Send *prosperity* now, my Lord.

¹²I will not forget You, for You are the One Who gives me the power to get wealth,

that Your covenant may be established. I have grace to *prosper.*

[13]Wealth and riches are in my house, I'm *blessed* for I fear You Lord.

[14]My labor in the Lord is not in vain, [15]and I increase in it.

[16]You increase my silver and my gold.

[17]I will leave an inheritance to my children's children, and the wealth of the wicked is laid up for me.

[18]I thank You, Lord, that You are bringing me into a wealthy place.

[19]Your blessing on my life makes me rich, and You add no sorrow to it. Your *blessing* is on me now!

[20]For I know the grace of my Lord, that though He was rich, yet for my sake He became poor, that I through His poverty might be made *rich.*

[21]I'm faithful and I abound in *blessing.*

[22]The hands of the diligent will be made rich. My hands are diligent.

[23]The Lord is my shepherd, and I shall not want, or lack.

[24]For the Lord God is a sun and shield; the Lord gives me grace and glory; no good thing will He withhold from me. I walk uprightly.

[25]Yes, He Who spared not His own Son, but delivered Him up for me, how shall He not with Him also freely give me all things?

[26]I have received abundance of grace, and the gift of righteousness; I reign in life as a king.

[27]I sow generously, and I reap generously. Father, I thank You that You make all grace to abound toward me, that I always have all sufficiency in all things. I have an *abundance* for every good work.

[28]I give and it is given back to me; good measure, pressed down, shaken together, and running over men give back to me.

[29]I seek first Your kingdom, and Your righteousness, and everything that the Gentile seeks is added to me.

[30]I'm redeemed from the curse of the law, and the *blessing* of Abraham has come upon me.

[31]All these *blessings* are upon me, and they are overtaking me:

I'm *blessed* in the city, and I'm *blessed* in the field, or in the country.

Blessed is the fruit of my body, and the fruit of my ground, and the fruit of my cattle, the *increase* of my family, and the flocks of my sheep.

My basket and my store is *blessed.*

I'm *blessed* when I come in, and I'm *blessed* when I go out.

The Lord has commanded the *blessing* upon me, in my bank account(s), and in all that I set my hand to.

He has *blessed* me in the land, which He has given me.

I have been established as a holy person unto my Lord. I'm holy and rich.

All the people of the earth shall see that I am called by the name of the Lord.

The Lord has made me *plenteous* in my goods, in the fruit of my body, and in the fruit of my cattle, and in the fruit of my ground, in the land, which He has given me.

Lord thank You that You have opened unto me Your good treasure, the Heavens, to give the rain unto my land in my season, and to *bless* all the work of my hands.

I will lend to many, and borrow from no one. I am the head and not the tail; and I am above only, and not beneath.

³²I'm a giver and a tither. The windows of heaven are open in my life, such *blessing* is being poured out upon me that I don't have room enough to contain it all, and the devourer has been rebuked

on my behalf.

³³Devil, take Your hands off my harvest, You have no place in that which the Lord has given to me. You have been rebuked.

³⁴The Lord came to give me *abundant* life, and there's nothing the devil can do about it.

³⁵He is under my feet!

³⁶I command money to come to me in abundance, and every resource that I need, I call it mine in Jesus name.

³⁷My God shall supply my every need according to His riches in Glory, by Christ Jesus.

³⁸I have more than enough.

³⁹I'm covered in the blood of Jesus,

⁴⁰and I am favored in this world.

⁴¹I'm always in the right place at the right time. All good deals come my way. I continually take a step further in that which God has for me. I'm stepping up!

⁴²I'm *increasing*!

⁴³I'm a soul winner ⁴⁴and a miracle worker! I am *blessed*, and it cannot be changed!

In the name of Jesus, Amen!

⁴⁵Father is hastening to perform His Word,

⁴⁶and His Holy angels are

going forth to bring it to pass!

References:

---

1 Genesis 39:3
2 Deuteronomy 29:9
3 Joshua 1:17
4 1 Kings 2:3
5 2 Chronicles 26:5
6 Psalm 1:3
7 Psalm 122:6
8 3 John 1:2
9 Job 36:11
10 Psalm 35:27
11 Psalm 118:25
12 Deuteronomy 8:18
13 Psalm 112:3
14 Isaiah 65:23,
    Psalm 127:1
15 Proverbs 13:11
16 Hosea 2:8
17 Proverbs 13:22
18 Psalm 66:12
19 Proverbs 10:22
20 2 Corinthians 8:9
21 Proverbs 28:20
22 Proverbs 10:4
23 Psalm 23:1
24 Psalm 34:10
25 Psalm 84:11
26 Romans 8:32
27 Romans 5:17
28 2 Corinthians 9:6-8
29 Luke 6:38
30 Matthew 6:33
31 Gal. 3:13-14
32 Deuteronomy 28:1-13
33 Malachi 3:10-11
34 Deuteronomy 33:27
35 John 10:10
36 Romans 16:20
37 2 Corinthians 9:11
38 Philippians 4:19
39 Exodus 36:5
40 Revelation 1:5
41 Luke 2:52
42 Romans 8:28
43 Psalm 115:14
44 Proverbs 11:30
45 John 14:12
46 Jeremiah 1:12

NOTES:_____

_____
_____
_____
_____
_____
_____
_____
_____
_____

Day Seven

THE HARVEST

To bring it all into perspective, let's now focus on what matters the most. Why did Jesus come, and why has the Word of God been given? Ultimately, it is for the sake of lost humanity. It is that the world may know the truth about God, and receive Him as Lord and Savior. The object of our faith should not rest in us alone, but should go far beyond us into the lives of those around us, and ultimately into the nations of the world.

---

¹Behold, now is the accepted time. Behold, now is the day of salvation.

²Whoever shall call upon the name of the Lord will be saved.

³For it is written, "As surely as I live,' says the Lord, 'every knee will bow before me; every tongue will acknowledge God.'"

⁴For with the heart a person believes, resulting in righteousness, and with the mouth he confesses, resulting in salvation.

⁵All the ends of the earth shall remember and turn to the LORD, and all the families of the nations shall worship before Him.

⁶Though Satan has blinded the minds of the unbelievers, to keep them from seeing the light of the gospel of the glory of Christ, Who is the image of God,

⁷that veil of deception is being removed!

⁸Blind eyes are opening!

⁹The true light is shining, and darkness is passing away.

¹⁰The abundance of the sea is being turned to my God.

¹¹It's harvest time! I lift up my eyes, and look on the fields; they are white already to harvest.

¹²And another angel came out of the temple, crying with a loud voice to Him that sat on the cloud, thrust in they sickle, and reap; for the time is come for thee to reap; for the harvest of the earth is ripe.

¹³Behold, the farmer waits for the precious fruit of the earth, and has long patience for it, until it receives the early and the latter rain.

¹⁴I ask of the LORD rain in the time of the latter rain; *so* the LORD will make bright clouds, and give me showers

of rain, and to every one grass in the field.

¹⁵The LORD is not slack concerning His promise, as some men count slackness; but is long-suffering toward us, not willing that any should perish, but that all should come to repentance.

¹⁶I am the voice of one crying in the wilderness, "Prepare ye the way of the Lord, make His paths straight."

¹⁷Jesus is coming!

¹⁸I am receiving the end of my faith, the salvation of souls. ¹⁹and I am rejoicing with joy unspeakable, and full of glory.

²⁰I am wise, capturing human lives for God, as a fisher of men—I gather and receive them for eternity.

²¹Jesus said He would make me to become a fisher of men.

²²Like Christ I'm seeking and saving that which is lost.

²³I believe in Jesus Christ, and as a result my family will be saved.

²⁴Nothing is impossible with God.

²⁵I have what I say, and my prayers are answered.

²⁶I love my neighbors, ²⁷and I call them heirs of salvation! Ministering angels go forth to minister to them.

²⁸Jesus said the harvest is great, but the laborers are few,

therefore, I pray for laborers to be sent out!

²⁹Father, thank You that You are drawing the lost, ³⁰and Your goodness is leading them to repentance.

³¹May they call on the only name given under Heaven by which they must be saved—the name of Jesus!

³²Who has heard such a thing? Who has seen such things? Shall the earth be made to bring forth in one day? Or shall a nation be born at once? For as soon as Zion travailed, she brought forth her children. Thank You Father that You bring to the place of birth, and You cause delivery as I travail in prayer for the lost.

³³You said, "Ask of Me and I shall give the nations *for* Your in inheritance; and the uttermost parts of the earth for Your possession. I ask for the nations.

³⁴God is willing that all be saved and come to the knowledge of the truth, therefore I pray for all men, I pray for those who are in authority; the leaders of governments around the world, that the gospel will spread unhindered throughout the nations.

³⁵Jesus was the Lamb of God, slain before the foundations of the world.

[36]The eternal sacrifice, [37]and He has made all nations of men of one blood to dwell on all the face of the earth, ordaining fore-appointed seasons and boundaries of their dwelling, to seek the Lord, if perhaps they might seek Him and find Him, thought indeed *He* is not far from each one of us.

[38]There is more joy in Heaven over one sinner who repents than over ninety-nine just persons who need no repentance. I will bring joy to all of Heaven by winning the lost.

[39]Through my obedience, many will be made righteous.

[40]I will shine like a star in heaven.

[41]Souls saved and disciples made are my glory and my joy.

[42]The salvation of God is sent to the nations, and they will heart it!

[43]The Spirit of the Lord is upon me, because He has anointed me to preach the gospel to the poor. He has sent me to heal the brokenhearted, to proclaim deliverance to the captives, and new sight to the blind, to set at liberty them that are bruised, to preach the acceptable year of the Lord.

In the name of Jesus, Amen!

References:

1 2 Corinthians 6:2
2 Romans 10:13
3 Romans 14:11
4 Romans 10:10
5 Psalm 22:27
6 2 Corinthians 4:4
7 2 Corinthians 4:3
8 Isaiah 42:7
9 1 John 2:8
10 Isaiah 60:5
11 John 4:35
12 Revelation 14:15
13 James 5:7
14 Zechariah 10:1
15 2 Peter 3:9
16 Mark 1:3
17 Revelation 3:11, 22:7, 22:12, 22:20
18 1 Peter 1:9
19 1 Peter 1:8
20 Proverbs 11:30
21 Mark 1:17
22 Luke 19:10
23 Acts 16:31
24 Luke 1:37
25 Mark 11:23, 24
26 Galatians 5:14
27 Hebrews 1:13-14
28 Matthew 9:37-38
29 John 6:44
30 Romans 2:4
31 Acts 4:12
32 Isaiah 66:8-9
33 Psalm 2:8
34 1 Timothy 2:1-4
35 Revelations 13:8
36 Hebrews 9:12
37 Acts 17:26-27

38 Luke 15:7   41 1 Thessalonians 2:20
39 Romans 5:19   42 Acts 28:28
40 Daniel 12:3   43 Luke 4:18-19

NOTES:_____

_____

_____

_____

_____

_____

_____

_____

_____

_____

_____

_____

_____

_____

_____

_____

_____

_____

_____

_____

_____

_____

_____

_____

_____

_____

_____

_____

_____

EPILOGUE & Free offer

I trust that your life has been enriched as you've spoken the Words of God, and have made them your personal confession. I encourage you to continue doing so. God's Word must be taken personally, and then it becomes significant. It isn't a storybook that we read, but rather a revelation of the will of God. It is His testament; old and new, and it must be received, believe, and acted upon.

To encourage you further, I'd like to offer you a free MP3 audio teaching about the power of your words, and how to "redeem the time!"

Go to this website to get your free copy now:
http://www.soul-purpose.org/bwj-book

If you would like to order additional copies of this guide, please email us at: books@soul-purpose.org, or you may visit http://soul-purpose.org/resources and order online.

Send your testimonies to: office@soul-purpose.org

God Bless!
Mike Van Buskirk

About Soul Purpose

Soul Purpose Ministries was founded in the year 2000 when Mike Van Buskirk took his first missionary trip to India. That first trip proved to be life changing, as Mike told the Lord he was willing to stay in India the rest of his life and serve Him. The Lord, it seems, accepted Mike's offer, and continues to use Mike and his family to bring the glorious message of Jesus to the nations of India and beyond.

On that first mission trip to India, in 2000, something else happened, which has made all these years of service in India possible. Mike met his wife Jyoti. In the mountains of Sikkim, India, she was there. They were married in August 2002, and now have two children.

Together, along with Jyoti's extended family in Sikkim, they have established a regional mission's base with three primary roles:

1. Church Planting
2. Ministry Training
3. Rescuing Children

From their home base in Sikkim they are reaching the nation of India and beyond; planting churches, training ministers and rescuing boys and girls from a life of uncertainty. The following is a picture of Mike and Jyoti with their team and their growing "Hope Home" family in Sikkim, India.

You can learn more by visiting their website:

http://soul-purpose.org

Mike is in the back – top right.
Jyoti (pronounced Jo tee) is on the right toward the front.
They are pictured here along with their "Hope Home"
children and staff.

Your purchase of *Breakfast With Jesus* helps support
Mike & Jyoti's ministry to the precious people of India.
Thank you!

SOUL PURPOSE MINISTRIES
http://soul-purpose.org

Made in the USA
Monee, IL
09 October 2023

44257983R00036